HOUGHTON MIFFLIN HARCOURT
TEXAS JOURNEYS

Program Authors

James F. Baumann · David J. Chard · Jamal Cooks
J. David Cooper · Russell Gersten · Marjorie Lipson
Lesley Mandel Morrow · John J. Pikulski · Héctor H. Rivera
Mabel Rivera · Shane Templeton · Sheila W. Valencia
Catherine Valentino · MaryEllen Vogt

Consulting Author
Irene Fountas

HOUGHTON MIFFLIN HARCOURT
School Publishers

Hello, Reader!

Do you know what it's like on the moon? Have you ever wondered where maple syrup comes from? Can you guess what it is like to travel in a donkey cart? In this book, you will discover the answers to these questions and more.

Open your book and see what discoveries are inside!

Sincerely,

The Authors

Exploring Together

Big Idea We discover new things every day.

Lesson 16

Words to Know 10

Background 12

Comprehension:
Main Ideas and Details 13

Let's Go to the Moon!
INFORMATIONAL TEXT 14
by Stephen R. Swinburne

Your Turn 35

I Read: June's Pictures 36

Mae Jemison BIOGRAPHY 44

Making Connections 47

Grammar/Write to Narrate 48

Lesson 17

Words to Know 52

Background 54

Comprehension: Compare and Contrast . . . 55

The Big Trip FANTASY 56
written and illustrated by Valeri Gorbachev

Your Turn 77

I Read: Plunk, Plunk 78

Lewis and Clark's Big Trip
INFORMATIONAL TEXT 86

Making Connections 89

Grammar/Write to Narrate 90

Lesson 18

Words to Know 94

Background 96

Comprehension: Author's Purpose 97

Where Does Food Come From? INFORMATIONAL TEXT 98
by Shelley Rotner and Gary Goss
photographed by Shelley Rotner

Your Turn 119

I Read: What Will We Do? 120

Jack and the Beanstalk FAIRY TALE 128

Making Connections 131

Grammar/Write to Narrate 132

Lesson

19

Words to Know 136

Background 138

Comprehension: Conclusions 139

Tomás Rivera

BIOGRAPHY 140

by Jane Medina • illustrated by René King Moreno

Your Turn 155

I Read: Fun with Gram 156

Life Then and Now INFORMATIONAL TEXT 164

Making Connections 167

Grammar/Reading-Writing Workshop
Personal Narrative 168

Lesson

20

Words to Know 172

Background 174

Comprehension: Cause and Effect 175

Little Rabbit's Tale

FOLKTALE 176

by Wong Herbert Yee
illustrated by Richard Bernal

Your Turn 195

I Read: A Springtime Rain 196

Silly Poems POEMS 204

Making Connections 207

Grammar/Reading-Writing Workshop
     Personal Narrative 208

Test POWER 212

POWER Practice 215

Words to Know G1

Glossary G2

Exploring Together

Unit 4

Big Idea

We discover new things every day.

Selections

Read Together	I Read	Read Together

Lesson **16**

 **Let's Go to the Moon!** Page 14

 June's Pictures Page 36

 **Mae Jemison** Page 44

Lesson **17**

  The Big Trip Page 56

 **Plunk, Plunk** Page 78

 **Lewis and Clark's Big Trip** Page 86

Lesson **18**

 Where Does Food Come From? Page 98

 **What Will We Do?** Page 120

 **Jack and the Beanstalk** Page 128

Lesson **19**

  **Tomás Rivera** Page 140

 **Fun with Gram** Page 156

 **Life Then and Now** Page 164

Lesson **20**

  Little Rabbit's Tale Page 176

 **A Springtime Rain** Page 196

 Silly Poems Page 204

Readers' Theater

Lesson 16

think

bring

before

light

because

carry

show

around

Vocabulary Reader

Context Cards

 TEKS 1.3H identify/read high-frequency words; **ELPS** 1F use accessible language to learn new language; 3B expand/internalize initial English vocabulary

10

Words to Know

Read Together

- ● Read each Context Card.
- ● Choose two blue words. Use them in sentences.

1

think

What do you think space is like?

2

bring

Spaceships can bring astronauts to space.

10, 9, 8, 7, 6, 5, 4, 3, 2, 1 . . . BLAST OFF!

The Flight

It can take four days to get to the Moon.
A rocket helps us blast into space. We ride
in the space ship at the top of the rocket.

We take a picture of our space ship, too.

Our flag is up!

Let's take one last look before we go. We see rocks and dust.

31

Let's Go Home

It's time to go back home.

What is it like to be on the Moon?
It's strange and fun at the same time.

When you look up and see the Moon, what do you think? Our Moon is beautiful!

1. In the story, the word <u>bring</u> means —

   ⬭ to show

   ⬭ to take

   ⬭ to clean

   TEKS 1.6C

2. ✔TARGET SKILL **Main Idea and Details**

   What do the astronauts do on the Moon?

   TEKS 1.14B, 1.24C, **ELPS** 4I

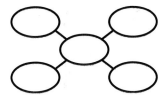

3. **Oral Language** Retell the order of events in **Let's Go to the Moon!** to a partner. Use the words from the story. Be sure to speak clearly. **TEKS** 1.14C, 1.28

TEKS **1.6C** use syntax/context to determine meaning; **1.14B** identify important facts/details; **1.14C** retell order of events; **1.24C** record information in visual formats; **1.28** share information/ideas by speaking clearly; **ELPS 4I** employ reading skills to demonstrate comprehension

June's
Pictures

June's Pictures

by Jolene Odegaard

June likes to take pictures. It is so much fun! She likes those cute little pigs.
Click, click, click.

Six cute dogs sit on steps.
June likes dogs.
Click, click, click.

Cats are cute when they nap.
Cats doze a lot! June likes cats.
Click, click, click.

That gull stands on a pole.
June likes gulls and sand dunes.
Click, click, click.

That mule is standing in a nice pose.
June likes mules.
Click, click, click.

The ducks have soft white plumes.
June likes ducks.
Click, click, click.

Bruce has a nice smile. Click. June will show Bruce this picture. June hopes Bruce will like it. Do you think he will?

Connect to Science

✔ **WORDS TO KNOW**

think	because
bring	carry
before	show
light	around

GENRE

A **biography** is a true story about events in a real person's life.

TEXT FOCUS

A **time line** shows the order of events. Use the time line on p. 46 to retell in order the important events in Mae Jemison's life.

 TEKS **1.3H** identify/read high-frequency words; **1.14C** retell order of events; **ELPS** **4F** use visual/contextual/peer/teacher support to read/comprehend texts

Mae Jemison

by Debbie O'Brien

Mae Jemison was born in Alabama. Mae knew she wanted to be a scientist when she grew up.

Mae studied very hard in college and became a doctor. She went to Africa because she wanted to help sick people there.

Here is Mae Jemison on the space shuttle. ▶

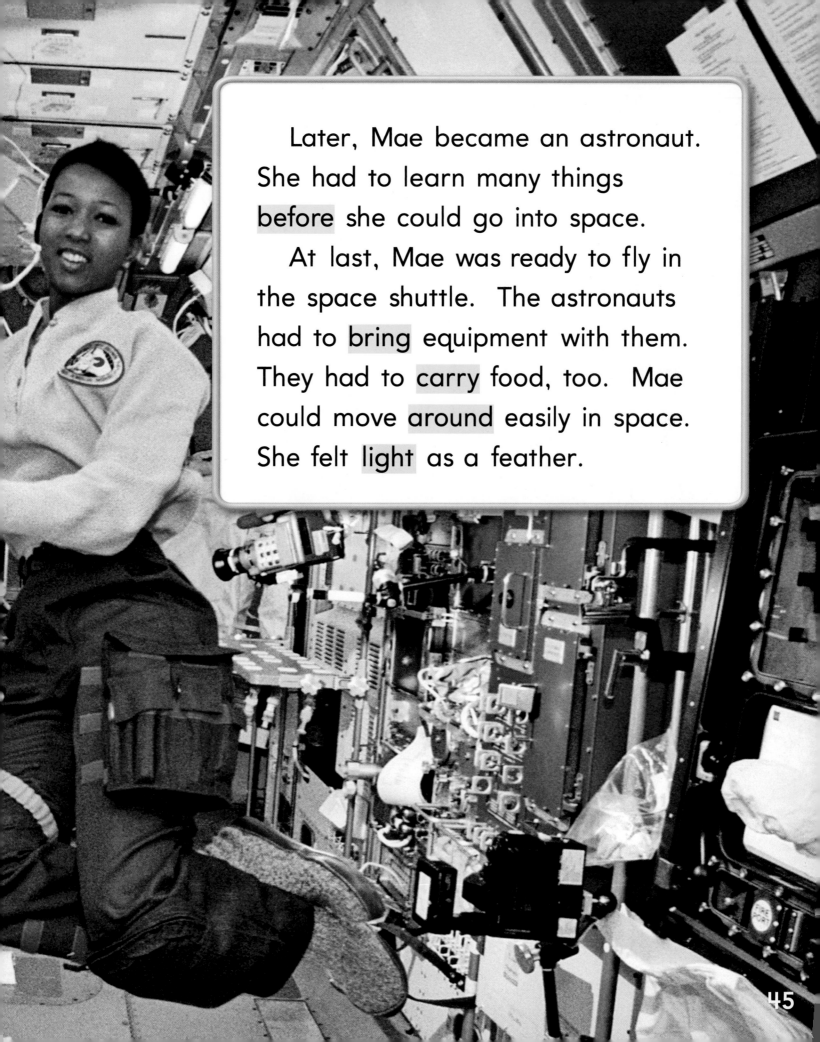

Later, Mae became an astronaut. She had to learn many things before she could go into space.

At last, Mae was ready to fly in the space shuttle. The astronauts had to bring equipment with them. They had to carry food, too. Mae could move around easily in space. She felt light as a feather.

Now Mae has her own company. She wants people to think about science. She tries to show people how science helps them every day.

Mae becomes a doctor.

Mae starts her company.

1980 1981   **1987**   **1993**   **1995**

Mae becomes an astronaut.

Making Connections

Text to Self

TEKS 1.19A, 1.19C, RC-1(F)

Connect to Science What if you were an astronaut? Write about what you would do in space.

Text to Text

TEKS 1.14A, 1.28, RC-1(F)

Tell Main Ideas Tell a partner the most important ideas you learned about being an astronaut. Speak clearly.

Text to World

TEKS 1.26, RC-1(F)

Draw and Share Find a picture of a real planet. Pretend that you have gone there. Draw a picture of things you discovered. Tell a partner about the planet.

 TEKS **1.14A** restate main idea; **1.19A** write brief compositions; **1.19C** write brief comments on texts; **1.26** create visual display/dramatization; **1.28** share information/ideas by speaking clearly; **RC-1(F)** make connections to experiences/texts/community; **ELPS** **1E** internalize new basic/academic language; **3G** express opinions/ideas/feelings; **3J** respond orally to information in media

Grammar Read Together

Questions A sentence that asks something is called a **question**. A question always begins with a capital letter and ends with a question mark.

> **W**hat is it like on the Moon**?**
> **A**re there any mountains**?**
> **D**o plants and animals live there**?**

Write each question correctly. Use another sheet of paper.

1. what do astronauts do on the Moon

2. do they wear space suits

3. can they jump really far

4. does their buggy go fast

5. why do they take pictures

Grammar in Writing

When you revise your writing, try using some questions.

TEKS **1.17C** revise drafts; **1.17D** edit drafts; **1.19A** write brief compositions; **1.21B(i)** capitalize beginning of sentences; **1.21C** recognize/use ending punctuation; **ELPS** **5G** narrate/describe/explain in writing

Write to Narrate

✔ **Ideas**   If you are writing **sentences** about yourself, be sure all your sentences are about one main idea.

Kim wrote about a cave she found. Later, she took out a sentence that didn't belong.

Revised Draft

My sister and I found a cave.

It was very dark inside.

~~I like the woods.~~

Writing Traits Checklist

✔ **Ideas**   Do all my sentences tell about one main idea?

✔ Does each sentence begin with a capital letter?

✔ Does each sentence end with the correct mark?

50

Look for the main idea in Kim's final copy.
Then revise your writing.   Use the Checklist.

Final Copy

A Big Surprise

My sister and I found a cave.

It was very dark inside.

We had a big surprise when some bats flew out!

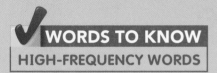

✓ **WORDS TO KNOW**
HIGH-FREQUENCY WORDS

there

by

sure

could

don't

car

about

maybe

Vocabulary
Reader

Context
Cards

TEKS **1.3H** identify/read high-frequency words;
ELPS **1F** use accessible language to learn new
language; **3B** expand/internalize initial English
vocabulary

Words to Know

Read Together

● Read each Context Card.

● Make up a new sentence that uses a blue word.

1

there

There are many ways to travel safely.

2

by

Wear a helmet when traveling by bike.

3 · sure

Be sure to buckle your seat belt!

4 · could

You could walk to the bus with a buddy.

5 · don't

Don't stand while the school bus is moving.

6 · car

A car should always stop at a STOP sign.

7 · about

These children know about bike safety.

8 · maybe

Maybe you can help someone be safe.

TEKS **1.3H** identify/read high-frequency words; **1.6D** categorize words; **ELPS 4D** use prereading supports to comprehend texts; **4F** use visual/contextual/peer/teacher support to read/comprehend texts

Background Read Together

✔ **WORDS TO KNOW** **Taking a Trip**

There are many ways to travel. You can go by bus, car, or train. Maybe you will go by plane. When you go, be sure to bring a book or a toy. It could be a long trip, and you don't want to be bored! Name some more ways to travel. Tell about them.

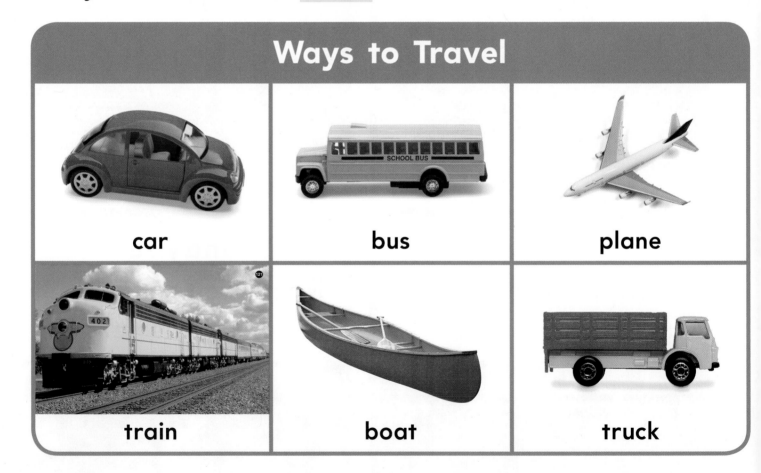

Ways to Travel

car

bus

plane

train

boat

truck

Comprehension

 **TARGET SKILL**   Compare and Contrast

When you **compare**, you tell how things are the same. When you **contrast**, you tell how things are different. How are the bike and car the same? How are they different?

bike   car

As you read **The Big Trip**, think about how the ways to travel are alike and different.

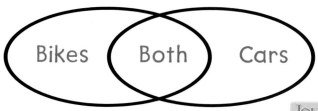

Bikes   Both   Cars

JOURNEYS DIGITAL **Powered by** DESTINATIONReading®
Comprehension Activities: Lesson 17

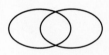

WORDS TO KNOW

there	don't
by	car
sure	about
could	maybe

TARGET SKILL

Compare and Contrast
Tell how two things are alike or not.

TARGET STRATEGY

Visualize Picture what is happening as you read.

GENRE

A **fantasy** is a story that could not happen in real life.

TEKS 1.4B ask questions/seek clarification/ locate details about texts; **RC-1(C)** monitor/ adjust comprehension; **ELPS 4K** employ analytical skills to demonstrate comprehension

Meet the Author and Illustrator

Valeri Gorbachev

Valeri Gorbachev says, "I love to draw for children and to create books when I am both author and illustrator." He also illustrates books for many other authors. To read more about Pig and Goat, look for **Where Is the Apple Pie?** and **One Rainy Day**.

The Big Trip

by
VALERI GORBACHEV

Essential Question

How are ways to travel the same and different?

"I am going to take a trip far away,"
Pig said to Goat one day.
"How will you go?" asked Goat.

"Let me think for a moment," said
Pig. "Maybe I will go by bike—that will
be a very nice trip."

"Oh, dear," said Goat. "You could
fall off a bike."

"Ah," said Pig. "Then I will drive a car."

60

"It's not a good idea, Pig," said Goat.
"A car can break down!"

"Oh," said Pig. "Then I will go by horse on my trip."

"I'm not sure about that," said Goat.
"Horses can be very jumpy!"

"Okay," said Pig. "Then I am going to
go by donkey cart—a donkey is very quiet."

"Not good, not good," said Goat.
"Donkeys can be very stubborn!"

 STOP AND THINK

Compare and Contrast
How do Pig and Goat each feel about taking a trip by donkey cart?

TEKS 1.9B, **ELPS** 4K

"Then I will go by train," said Pig.

1. In the story, the word <u>don't</u> means —

⬭ finished

⬭ do not

⬭ dark

TEKS 1.6C

2. 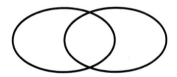 **Compare and Contrast**

How are Pig and Goat the same?
How are they different? **TEKS** 1.9B

3. Oral Language Take turns telling the story with a partner. Tell the events in order.

TEKS 1.9A; **ELPS** 3H, 4G

 TEKS **1.6C** use syntax/context to determine meaning, **1.9A** retell story events, **1.9B** describe/analyze characters; **ELPS** **3H** narrate/describe/explain with detail; **4G** demonstrate comprehension through shared reading/retelling/responding/note-taking

Plunk, Plunk

✓ **PHONICS SKILL**

Long **e: e, ee, ea**
Final **ng, nk**

✓ **WORDS TO KNOW**

there
sure

TEKS **1.3A(i)** decode words with consonants; **1.3A(ii)** decode words with vowels; **1.3A(v)** decode words with vowel digraphs; **1.3C(ii)** decode using open syllables; **1.3C(iv)** decode using VCe pattern; **1.3H** identify/read high-frequency words; **ELPS** **4A** learn English sound-letter relationships/decode

78

Plunk, Plunk

by Charles Barker

illustrated by Karen Stormer Brooks

Plunk, plunk! Drop, drop!
Drops fall on Frank's cheek.
What made those drops?

A green hose is in the green grass. Frank thinks it made the drops. He is sure it did.

The green hose leads Frank to this big tree trunk.

"Who is back there? I think it's Jean. Is it? Is it Jean?" asks Frank.

"Yes, Frank. It's me. Did you get wet?" asks Jean. "I hope you think it was fun."

Look for words that tell where and when in Sam's final copy. Then revise your own writing. Use the Checklist.

Final Copy

Our Camping Trip

My family went camping.

First, we set up our new tent by a lake.

The next day I was so happy because we rode in a canoe!

93

✔ **WORDS TO KNOW**
HIGH-FREQUENCY WORDS

food
first
ground
sometimes
under
these
right
your

Vocabulary
Reader

Context
Cards

 TEKS 1.3H identify/read high-frequency words; **ELPS** 1F use accessible language to learn new language; 3B expand/internalize initial English vocabulary

94

Words to Know

Read Together

- Read each Context Card.

- Ask a question that uses one of the blue words.

1

food

All kinds of food can grow in a garden.

2

first

The seeds are planted in the soil first.

3 **ground**

Keep the ground near the plants wet.

4 **sometimes**

Sometimes pumpkins grow very big!

5 **under**

Carrots grow under the ground.

6 **these**

These tomatoes are ready to be picked.

7 **right**

You can pick pea pods right off of the vine.

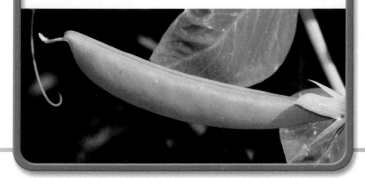

8 **your**

What will you plant in your garden?

Background

✔ **WORDS TO KNOW**   **From Farm to Table**

Do you know where your food comes from?
Many fruits and vegetables grow on farms.
First, farmers plant seeds. Some plants,
like carrots, grow under the ground.
Others, like beans, grow above the ground.
Farmers pick these vegetables at the right
time. Sometimes they send them to stores
for us to buy.

TEKS 1.4C establish purpose/monitor comprehension; **1.13** identify topic/explain author's purpose; **RC–1(A)** establish reading purposes
ELPS **1E** internalize new basic/academic language; **4F** use visual/contextual/peer/teacher support to read/comprehend texts

Comprehension

Read Together

✔ **TARGET SKILL** Author's Purpose

Authors write for many reasons. They write to share a message or to make you laugh. They write to tell facts and details to help you learn something.

wheat

As you read **Where Does Food Come From?**, think about why the authors wrote the story.

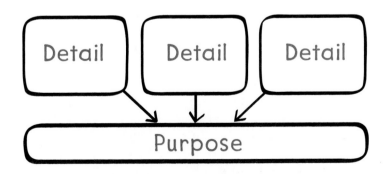

Detail   Detail   Detail

Purpose

Where Does **Food** Come From?

Shelley Rotner and Gary Goss

Photographs by Shelley Rotner

✔ WORDS TO KNOW

food	under
first	these
ground	right
sometimes	your

✔ TARGET SKILL

Author's Purpose Tell why an author writes a book.

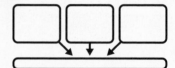

✔ TARGET STRATEGY

Summarize Stop to tell important ideas as you read.

GENRE

Informational text gives facts about a topic.

TEKS **1.13** identify topic/explain author's purpose; **1.14B** identify important facts/details; **1.14C** retell order of events; **ELPS** **4G** demonstrate comprehension through shared reading/retelling/responding/note-taking

Meet the Author and Photographer

Shelley Rotner

Shelley Rotner started writing books about things that interested her daughter. If you have questions about the world around you, the answers might well be in a book by Ms. Rotner!

Meet the Author

Gary Goss

Gary Goss says, "I love food and creating. I also love working with kids." Gary has written a children's cookbook called **Blue Moon Soup**.

Corn is grain that grows in fields.
Popcorn is made from corn.
First you heat it, and then it pops.

Wait! That's not right! It
doesn't wail! It huffs and puffs!
Huff, huff, huff! Puff, puff, puff!

No, no, no! You must be
mixed up. Beasts don't huff and
puff. Beasts wail!

Well, sometimes beasts huff
and puff. This beast huffs and
puffs. This beast huffs and puffs
and chases YOU!

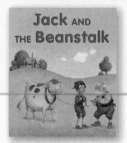

Jack AND THE Beanstalk

Connect to Traditional Tales

✔ **WORDS TO KNOW**

food	under
first	these
ground	right
sometimes	your

GENRE

A **fairy tale** is an old story with characters that can do amazing things.

TEXT FOCUS

Many fairy tales end with **storytelling phrases**, such as **happily ever after**. Find these words. Why do you think the storyteller uses them?

TEKS **1.7A** connect stories/fables to personal experiences; **1.7B** understand recurring phrases in traditional tales; **ELPS** **4I** employ reading skills to demonstrate comprehension

Jack AND THE Beanstalk

Once upon a time, there was a boy named Jack. He and his mom had no money for food because someone had taken their goose. Sometimes, it would lay golden eggs for them!

Jack went to sell their cow. He met a man. "I will trade these special beans for your cow," the man said.

Jack came home. His mother was mad. She threw the beans on the ground.

Soon a tall beanstalk grew. Jack climbed it. At the top was a huge castle. Inside, Jack found his goose in a cage under a table!

Then Jack heard, "FEE! FIE! FOE! FUM! Look out! Here I come!"

It was a giant! First Jack grabbed the goose. Then he ran right out the door.

Jack climbed down the beanstalk
as fast as he could. He chopped
it down.

Now Jack and his mother were
safe, and they had their goose.
They all lived happily ever after.

Making Connections

 **Read Together**

 Text to Self   TEKS 1.19A, RC-1(F)

Write a List Make a list of foods you like to eat. Tell classmates about them.

 Text to Text   TEKS 1.28, RC-1(F)

Tell About Food Jack's beanstalk started out as tiny beans. Describe to a partner beans and other vegetables you have eaten.

 Text to World   TEKS 1.24A,1.24C, RC-1(F)

Connect to Technology Use the Internet to find out how people grow your favorite food. Draw a picture that shows what you learned.

 TEKS **1.19A** write brief compositions; **1.24A** gather evidence; **1.24C** record information in visual formats; **1.28** share information/ideas by speaking clearly; **RC-1(F)** make connections to experiences/texts/community; **ELPS** **3H** narrate/describe/explain with detail; **5B** write using new basic/content-based vocabulary

Grammar Read Together

Names of Months, Days, and
Holidays The names of **months** in a year,
days of the week, and **holidays** begin with
a capital letter. When you write a date, use
a **comma** between the day of the month
and the year.

Names of Months

We planted seeds on **M**ay 14, 2011.

Days of Week

My dad cooked soup on **F**riday.

Holidays

My family eats turkey on **T**hanksgiving.

Write each sentence correctly. Use another sheet of paper. Tell a partner what you did to correct each sentence.

1. Ali began school on september 8 2010.

2. She has science club every friday.

3. There was no school on memorial day.

4. Last wednesday our class took a field trip.

5. School ended on june 14 2011.

Grammar in Writing

When you proofread your writing, be sure you have written the names of months, days, and holidays correctly.

Write to Narrate

Read Together

☑ **Sentence Fluency** A good **friendly letter** is not boring! Use different kinds of sentences to make your writing lively and interesting.

Ned drafted a letter about a special meal he had. Then he added a question.

Revised Draft

Then we tasted all the food.
Can you guess my favorite?
ʌ The apple pie was best of all.

Writing Traits Checklist

☑ **Sentence Fluency** Did I write different kinds of sentences?

☑ Does my letter have all five parts?

☑ Did I use capital letters and commas correctly?

Look for different kinds of sentences in Ned's final copy. Then revise your writing. Use the Checklist.

Final Copy

March 8, 2010

Dear Mario,

My school had a potluck supper. First, each class cooked something. Then we tasted all the food. Can you guess my favorite? The apple pie was best of all.

Your friend,

Ned

WORDS TO KNOW
HIGH-FREQUENCY WORDS

work

great

talk

paper

were

soon

laugh

done

Vocabulary Reader

Context Cards

TEKS 1.3H identify/read high-frequency words; **ELPS** 1F use accessible language to learn new language; 3B expand/internalize initial English vocabulary

Words to Know

Read Together

● **Read each** Context Card.

● Use a blue word to tell a story about a picture.

1

work

People go to work every day.

2

great

She did a great job baking this cake!

3
talk
He likes to talk with customers at his job.

4
paper
This artist does his work on paper.

5
were
The farmers were very busy today.

6
soon
Soon it will be time to go to lunch.

7
laugh
A silly clown makes everyone laugh.

8
done
He goes home when the work is done.

Background   Read Together

✓ **WORDS TO KNOW** **Writing a Book** Most books begin with an idea. Sometimes a writer talks about the idea with a friend. If the idea is funny, the writer hopes the friend laughs! Soon it is time to start writing. A writer may write on paper. It is a lot of work. It feels great when the book is done. What kind of book would you write if you were a writer?

Things a Writer Uses

books

computer

printer

pencil

paper

TEKS 1.4C establish purpose/monitor comprehension; **1.14B** identify important facts/details; **RC–1(A)** establish reading purposes; **RC-1(D)** make inferences/use textual evidence; **ELPS 1E** internalize new basic/academic language; **4F** use visual/contextual/peer/teacher support to read/ comprehend texts

Comprehension  Read Together

✓ **TARGET SKILL** Conclusions

Good readers use details to figure out things about a story that an author may not tell them. This is called drawing **conclusions**. Readers use details from the text, pictures, and what they know from their own life to draw conclusions.

What is your conclusion?
What clues helped you?

As you read **Tomás Rivera**, use story clues and what you already know to draw conclusions.

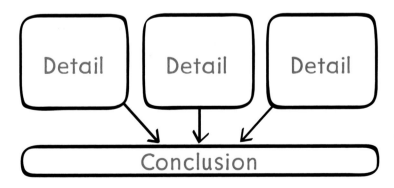

✔ **WORDS TO KNOW**

work	were
great	soon
talk	laugh
paper	done

✔ **TARGET SKILL**

Conclusions Use details to figure out more about the text.

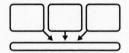

✔ **TARGET STRATEGY**

Monitor/Clarify Find ways to figure out what doesn't make sense.

GENRE

A **biography** tells about a real person's life.

TEKS **1.4B** ask questions/seek clarification/ locate details about texts; **1.4C** establish purpose/monitor comprehension; **RC-1(C)** monitor/adjust comprehension; **RC-1(D)** make inferences/ use textual evidence

Meet the Author

Jane Medina

Just like Tomás Rivera, Jane Medina is both a teacher and a writer. She began writing poems when she was a teenager. Since then, she has written books that have poems in both Spanish and English.

Meet the Illustrator

René King Moreno

As a young girl, René King Moreno loved to draw and paint. She also loved going to the library. She studied art in school, and now she illustrates children's books.

Tomás Rivera

by Jane Medina

illustrated by
René King Moreno

Essential Question

What clues help
you figure out how
characters feel?

141

Tomás Rivera was born in Texas.
Tomás and his family went from
place to place picking crops.

Tomás helped pick crops all day. It was
a lot of work. When the work was
done, Tomás would talk with his Grandpa.

"Come quick!" Grandpa called.
"It's time for stories!"

"You tell the best stories!"
Tomás said. "I wish I could
tell great stories, too."

The next day, Grandpa said, "We can
get lots of stories for you, Tomás."
"When?" asked Tomás.

Joan can't wait to go to Gram's.
She knows it will be fun. So far,
they've cut rows of paper dolls.
What's next?

Gram shows Joan a huge, oak
trunk. It's loaded with things. Joan
sees coats and hats and a dress.

"Gram," she asks, "where did
you get this green silk dress?"
"It's from Pops. Put it on."
Gram and Joan laugh.

Gram's green dress is so soft. The silk floats around Joan. Gram's face glows. Joan looks nice.

Joan takes off the dress. Then
she sees a green silk hat. She puts
it on. It fits!

Mom and Rob come in. Gram tells
Rob to see what Pops left in the trunk.
Rob sees a big tan hat and a gray vest.

"Oh, no! The sky is falling!" yells
Little Rabbit.
"The sky is not falling," laughs
Mother Rabbit. "An apple just fell
from the apple tree!"

"I didn't get to catch a fish," says Goose.
"I didn't get to eat my snack," says Beaver.
"I didn't get to sleep," says Turtle.

We like rain. We are glad when
it rains. It's fun to be out in a
springtime rain.

Kay likes to walk her dog in the rain. Rain can wash pathways and make them clean.

Kay sees raindrops shine on plants. Rain helps plants grow and spread.

Dad takes Quinn to class. Quinn is dressed for rain. He has his raincoat. He has a matching rain hat on his head.

When it rains a lot, we stay in. Swings and slides get wet, so we can't use them. We get a long playtime in class.

Jane peeks out. She sees raindrops on the glass. Jane looks up.

"Quick!" Jane yells. "You must see this!"

Making Connections

Text to Self
TEKS 1.19A, RC-1(F)

Silly Sentences Write sentences to tell classmates about something silly that you saw or did.

Text to Text
TEKS 1.20A(iii), 1.27A, 1.29, RC-1(F)

Use Describing Words Think of the rabbits in the selections. Take turns with a partner. Tell what the story rabbit and a real rabbit look like.

Text to World
TEKS 1.15B, 1.24A, 1.24C, RC-1(F)

Connect to Social Studies Find out where apples grow. Use the symbols on a map. Tell what you find out, using words like **north**, **south**, **east**, or **west**.

TEKS 1.15B explain signs/symbols; **1.19A** write brief compositions; **1.20A(iii)** understand/use adjectives; **1.24A** gather evidence; **1.24C** record information in visual formats; **1.27A** listen attentively/ask relevant questions; **1.29** follow discussion rules; **RC-1(F)** make connections to experiences/texts/community; **ELPS 2I** demonstrate listening comprehension of spoken English

Grammar

Prepositions A preposition is a word that joins with other words to help explain where something is or when it happens. A **prepositional phrase** is a group of words that starts with a preposition.

The rabbit napped **under** a tree.
It was **before the apple fell**.

Read each sentence with a partner. Find the preposition or prepositional phrase in each sentence. Write them on another sheet of paper. Talk with your partner to decide whether the preposition tells about where or when something happened.

1. Ted read a book before dinner.

2. He was in an apple tree.

3. There was a sound above his head.

4. A bird flew around him.

5. He was right by its nest!

Grammar in Writing

When you revise your writing, be sure to include prepositional phrases to tell about where and when.

TEKS **1.17C** revise drafts; **1.17D** edit drafts; **1.18A** write brief stories; **1.20A(vii)** understand/use time-order transition words; **ELPS** **5G** narrate/describe/explain in writing

Reading-Writing Workshop: Revise

Write to Narrate

✓ **Word Choice**   In a good **personal narrative**, exact details help readers picture what happened.

Ava wrote about a special day. Later, she changed words to make them more exact.

Revised Draft

Then we went to a museum.

rocks, stars, and dinosaurs

I saw ~~stuff~~.
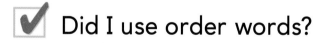

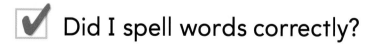 **Revising Checklist**

✓ Do my sentences have exact details?

✓ Did I use order words?

✓ Did I spell words correctly?

Look for details in Ava's final copy. Then revise your own writing. Use the Checklist.

Final Copy

A Great Day

Last Friday, my mom and I had an adventure. First, we took a bus to the city. Then we went to a museum. I saw rocks, stars, and dinosaurs. Last, we gladly ate some apples in the park.

Read the story. Then read each question. Choose the best answer for the question.

A Very Cold Place

Some people like the North Pole. It takes a long time to get there. You can get near the North Pole by boat or by plane, but you still have to walk to get there.

People get around by sled. The sleds are pulled by special dogs. Their fur is very thick.

If you go to the North Pole, you will see a lot of snow. You might also see polar bears on the way. Seals live there, too. You might even see a whale or two!

1 What is the North Pole like?

- ⬭ Hot
- ⬭ Rainy
- ⬭ Cold

2 Look at these pictures.

Picture 1   **Picture 2**   **Picture 3**

Which picture shows a way to get near the North Pole?

- ⬭ Picture 1
- ⬭ Picture 2
- ⬭ Picture 3

3 What animals might you see at the North Pole?

- ⬭ Polar bears, seals, and whales
- ⬭ Polar bears and tigers
- ⬭ Polar bears and cats

GO ON ▶

Ice-Cold Fish

The ocean near the South Pole is like a big bowl of ice and water. The water is so cold, bits of ice <u>float</u> on top of the water. More than ninety kinds of fish live there. One of them is the ice fish. Ice fish live in cold, cold water. Blood would freeze in this water. Ice fish have something that stops their blood from freezing. This lets them swim in the very icy water.

1 What is this story mostly about?
- ⬭ Ice fish
- ⬭ Cold water
- ⬭ Swimming

2 Where do ice fish live?
- ⬭ On top of the ice
- ⬭ In icy water
- ⬭ In a fish tank

3 The word <u>float</u> means to —
- ⬭ swim under
- ⬭ stay on top
- ⬭ sink down

STOP

POWER Practice

Lesson 16

Ask Questions 216

Spelling 218

Media Techniques 220

Lesson 17

Signs and Symbols 222

Sorting Words 224

Spelling 226

Taking Notes 228

Lesson 18

Writing a Letter 230

Spelling 232

Making a Chart 234

Lesson 19

Follow Directions 236

Asking Questions 238

Spelling 240

Using a Bar Graph 242

Lesson 20

Publishing 244

Compound Words 246

ABC Order 248

Using a Diagram 250

Ask Questions

You can ask questions to get more information about something. When you ask a question, a question word such as **who, what, where, when, why,** or **how** often comes first. Sometimes a verb comes first. The words in the answer often change order.

Question	Answer
What **is** the nearest **star**?	The nearest **star is** the Sun.
Where **is** the **book**?	The **book is** in my desk.
Will the **moon** be full tonight?	The **moon will** be full tonight.
Can I use the telescope?	**I can** use the telescope.

TEKS 1.4B ask questions/seek clarification/locate details about texts; 1.20C ask questions with subject-verb inversions;
ELPS 5D edit writing for standard grammar and usage

Look at the picture. Write two questions about the picture. Check that the words are in an order that makes sense. Trade papers with a partner. Write answers to the questions.

Spelling

CVCe Words

Read these words.

June   bike   mile

stone   white   tube

In each of these words, the first vowel has a long vowel sound. The **e** at the end of the word is silent.

Follow each step. Write the word on a sheet of paper. Read the word.

1. Start with | h | o | p |.

2. Add | e | to the end.

3. Change | p | to | l |.

TEKS 1.3B apply letter-sound knowledge to create words; 1.15A follow written multi-step directions; 1.21A form letters legibly; 1.22B (ii) spell CVCe words; ELPS 5C spell English words with increasing accuracy

4. Change h to m .

5. Change o to i .

6. Change m to w   h .

7. Change w   h to s   m .

Handwriting

Write the sentences below neatly on a sheet of paper. Form the letters carefully. Put a pencil space between each word.

I watched a mole come out of a hole. It made me smile.

Media Techniques

Media are ways of communicating with many people. A book is a kind of media. When you read a book you may imagine moving pictures, voices, or other sounds to help you understand the words.

Television, computers, CDs, radio, and movies are other forms of media. They use movement and sound to give information. Characters on TV move and talk. Music can make you feel a certain way. An advertisement on the Internet may use sound to get your attention.

TEKS 1.16B identify media techniques; ELPS 2F listen to/derive meaning from media; 3J respond orally to information in media

Work with a partner. Talk about what you have seen or heard in computer programs, television shows, movies, or advertisements.

Choose one computer program or one advertisement.

Make a list of the sounds you hear.

- Are there voices or music?

- Are there other sounds, such as ringing bells, sizzling, or crunching?

Make a list of the movement you see.

- Are people or things moving?

- Does the picture that you see change in any way?

Think about how the sounds and movements help you understand what you are watching.

TEKS 1.15A follow written multi-step directions

Signs and Symbols

Read Together

Follow the directions below. Trace the path with your finger.

1. Start at the tree.

2. Go right 2 squares. ➡

3. Go down 1 square. ⬇

4. Stop at the stop sign.

TEKS 1.15A follow written multi-step directions; 1.15B explain signs/symbols; **ELPS** 3E share information in cooperative learning interactions

Now work with a partner. Tell your partner how to get to another place on the map. Trace the path with your finger. Then switch roles.

Make your own map.

- On a piece of paper, draw nine boxes.

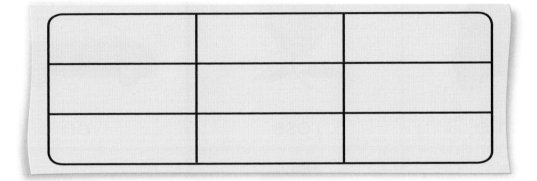

- Place a different symbol or sign in four of the boxes. Here are some ideas for symbols.

Explain what each symbol or sign stands for. Then tell your partner how to get to a place on your map.

Sorting Words

Grouping things that are alike helps you better understand words.

Animals	Plants	Things That Go
turtle	rose	van
lion	tree	truck

1. Make a chart like this one.

Animals	Plants	Things That Go

TEKS 1.6D categorize words; ELPS 1C use strategic learning techniques to acquire vocabulary

2. Look at each word below. Some words belong on the chart and some do not.

9 nine	car	bus	1 one
daisy	rabbit	boat	carrot
bird	2 two	bear	5 five

3. Write the words in the correct group on your chart.

4. Which words are left over? What group do they belong to?

Add more words to your chart.

Spelling  Read Together

Consonant Blends

Many words have two consonants next to each other. Write the new words below.

Start with **lip**.
Put **s** in front of the **l**.
The new word is **slip**.

Start with **mile**.
Put **s** in front of the **m**.
The new word is **smile**.

Start with **fog**.
Put **r** after the **f**.
The new word is **frog**.

Start with **tap**.
Put **r** after the **t**.
The new word is **trap**.

TEKS **1.21A** form letters legibly; **1.22B(iii)** spell words with consonant blends; **ELPS 5C** spell English words with increasing accuracy

Handwriting  Read Together

Write each of these words neatly on a sheet of paper. Form the letters carefully.

| **lap** | **nap** | **well** | **tick** | **pot** |

Now write the words again with an **s** in front of each one. Read the words.

Write these sentences neatly. Put a pencil space between each word. Put two pencil spaces between the sentences.

When the truck driver saw
the frog, he stopped the
truck. The frog hopped away.

Taking Notes

When you **take notes**, write words to help you remember what you read, see, or hear.

Look at the pictures.

TEKS 1.24C record information in visual formats; ELPS 1C use strategic learning techniques to acquire vocabulary

Make a chart like this one. Use the chart to take notes about each picture.

Notes about Ways to Go			
	tricycle	car	bike
How many wheels does it have?			
What makes it move?			

How are tricycles, cars, and bikes alike? How are they different?

Use your notes to write the answers.

Writing a Letter

You can write a letter to tell about something you have done. When you write a letter, be sure you have all the parts.

Heading ——————————— February 2, 2010

Greeting —— Dear Lily,

Body —— It was hot today! First we went for a swim. Then we made a sand castle. Last we had ice-cold lemonade. I miss you. I hope you are having fun in your new snowy home!

Closing ——————————— Love,

Signature ——————————— Hank

TEKS 1.19B write short letters; **1.20A (vii)** understand/use time-order transition words; **ELPS** 5G narrate/describe/explain in writing

Write a letter to a friend. Tell about something fun you did. Be sure to tell the events in order. Use words such as **first, next,** and **last** to make your writing clear. Remember to use the five parts of a letter. When you are finished, read your letter to a partner.

Spelling

Read Together

Consonant Blends

Many words have two consonants next to each other. Write the new words below.

Start with **rip**.

Put **d** in front of the **r**.

The new word is **drip**.

Start with **rack**.

Put **c** in front of the **r**.

The new word is **crack**.

Start with **rain**.

Put **t** in front of the **r**.

The new word is **train**.

Start with **top**.

Put **s** in front of the **t**.

The new word is **stop**.

TEKS 1.27B follow/restate/give oral instructions; **ELPS** 2E use support to enhance/confirm understanding of spoken language; 2I demonstrate listening comprehension of spoken English

3. Continue giving directions that will help your partner draw.

4. Have your partner repeat what you say or ask questions, if needed.

5. Have your partner guess what the picture is.

6. Switch roles with your partner. Follow your partner's directions.

7. Write sentences that tell about the pictures.

This bus takes me to school.

Asking Questions

When you don't understand something you can ask questions. The answers can help make the information clear.

Remember, when you ask questions a verb or question word often comes first.

Question	Answer
What **can we** do?	**We can** pick oranges.
Will we fill the box?	**We will** fill the box.

TEKS 1.4B ask questions/seek clarification/locate details about texts; **ELPS** 3E share information in cooperative learning interactions

Look at the picture. Think about what the people in the picture are doing.

On a sheet of paper, write two questions about the picture. Make sure that the words are in an order that makes sense. Then talk with a partner to help each other answer the questions. How else could you answer the questions?

Spelling

Consonant Blends

Many words have two or three consonants next to each other. Write the new words below.

Start with **rack**.
Put **c** in front of the **r**.
The new word is **crack.**

Start with **lash**.
Put **sp** in front of the **l**.
The new word is **splash**.

Start with **ripe**.
Put **st** in front of the **r**.
The new word is **stripe**.

TEKS **1.17E** publish/share writing; **1.27A** listen attentively/ask relevant questions; **1.29** follow discussion rules

Class Discussions

When you and your classmates are deciding what to call the class book, be sure to follow these rules for discussion.

- Look at the person who is talking.

- Listen carefully.

- Raise your hand. Wait to be called on to talk.

- Stay on topic when you speak.

- Speak clearly.

- Do not speak too fast or too slow.

- Speak in complete sentences.

Take turns reading the class book to each other.

Compound Words

Read
Together

A word made from two smaller words is called
a **compound word**.

sun + **flower** = **sunflower**

A sunflower is a flower that is bright yellow,
like the sun.

ant + **hill** = **anthill**

An anthill is a hill of sand where ants live.

TEKS **1.3F** identify/read compound words; **1.6B** determine meaning of compound words; **ELPS** **1F** use accessible language to learn new language

Find the compound words in these sentences.

1. We like to play basketball at the playground.

2. Meg spilled her popcorn in the sandbox.

3. I have something in my backpack.

Write the compound words on a sheet
of paper. Read them to a partner.
Then explain to your partner what each
compound word means.

Make more compound words with your partner.
The words in this box may help you.

sun	set	rain	bow	moon
beam	shine	light	night	fall

247

ABC Order

Read Together

Write these words on another sheet of paper.

rain   umbrella   puddle   splash   drop

Circle the first letter of each word. Use the
first letter to write the words in ABC order.
Write neatly from left to right and from the
top of the page to the bottom.

TEKS 1.6E alphabetize/use dictionary; 1.21A form letters legibly

Write these words on your paper.

puddle   pig   panda   potato   peach

These words all begin with the letter **p**. To write them in ABC order, look at the next letter. Circle the second letter in each word. Use the second letter to write the words in ABC order.

Remember to write neatly so others can read your work.

Using a Diagram

A **diagram** is a picture that helps explain how something works, how it changes, or how it is put together. It also has words to help explain the pictures.

Read the following information.

1. A butterfly lays an **egg** on a leaf.

2. The egg hatches into a **caterpillar**.

3. The caterpillar grows.

4. The caterpillar forms a **chrysalis.**

5. A **butterfly** comes out of the chrysalis.

This diagram shows how a butterfly grows from an egg.

1 A butterfly lays an **egg** on a leaf.

2 The egg hatches into a **caterpillar**.

3 The caterpillar grows.

4 The caterpillar forms a **chrysalis**.

5 A **butterfly** comes out of the chrysalis.

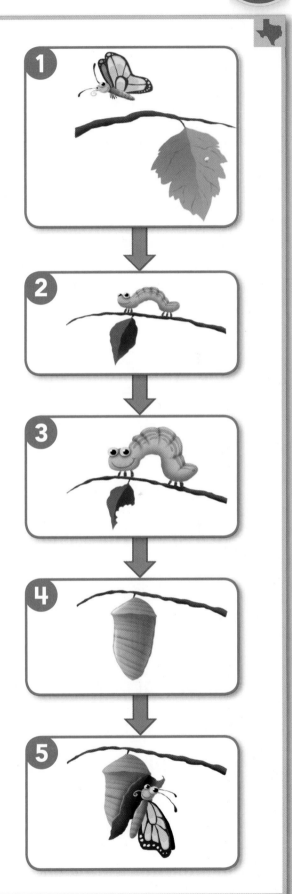

TEKS 1.24C record information in visual formats; ELPS 1C use strategic learning techniques to acquire vocabulary

On a separate sheet of paper, draw a diagram that shows how frogs grow from eggs. Use this information.

1. Frogs lay **eggs** in ponds.

2. The eggs hatch into **tadpoles**.

3. Tadpoles grow into **frogs**.

Draw arrows to show how one stage changes into the next. You can use the words **eggs, tadpoles,** and **frogs** to label your diagram.

Share your diagram with your classmates.

Words to Know

Unit 4   High-Frequency Words

16 Let's Go to the Moon!

think	because
bring	carry
before	show
light	around

17 The Big Trip

there	don't
by	car
sure	about
could	maybe

18 Where Does Food Come From?

food	under
first	these
ground	right
sometimes	your

19 Tomás Rivera

work	were
great	soon
talk	laugh
paper	done

20 Little Rabbit's Tale

want	more
old	wash
try	mother
use	door

Glossary

A

apple

An **apple** is a fruit with red, yellow, or green skin. Jose´ picked a red **apple** from that tree.

B

beaver

A **beaver** is an animal that has large front teeth and a flat tail. We saw a **beaver** swimming in the water.

born

Born means brought to life. The kittens were **born** yesterday.

C

chocolate

Chocolate is a kind of food that is dark and sweet. **Chocolate** is my favorite kind of candy.

crater

A **crater** is a large hole in the ground. We saw a picture of a big **crater** on the Moon.

D

desert

A **desert** is a large dry area of land. The **desert** has a lot of sand.

E

engine

An **engine** is a kind of machine that burns oil, gas, or wood. My sister's car has an **engine** that makes it go very fast.

exclaimed

To **exclaim** means to say something in a strong way. "Watch out!" Dillon **exclaimed**.

F

family

A **family** is a group of people who often live together. Our **family** lives in the city.

favorite

Favorite means what you like the most. My **favorite** pet is a dog.

footprints

A **footprint** is the mark a person or an animal leaves. We looked back and saw our **footprints** in the sand.

G

goose

A **goose** is a kind of bird that has a long neck. The **goose** is sitting on her nest.

gravity

Gravity is the force that pulls us to the ground. The **gravity** is stronger on Earth than it is on the Moon.

H

happily ever after

Happily ever after is a storytelling phrase that means happy from that time on. The three little pigs lived **happily ever after**.

hooray

Hooray is a word that people shout when they are happy. When Jim won the race, we all yelled **hooray**!

I

island

An **island** is an area of land that has water all around it. Risa and her family took a boat to the **island**.

J

jumpy

Jumpy means moving in a way that isn't smooth. Tino moved in a **jumpy** way that made him spill his milk.

L

library
A **library** is a place where books are kept. I borrow a book from the **library** each Monday.

lunar
Lunar means having to do with the Moon. My grandpa remembers watching the first **lunar** landing on TV.

O

oh
Oh is a word that shows strong feelings. "**Oh** no!" said Mom when the car did not start.

P

paddy
A **paddy** is a field of rice. The people worked hard in the rice **paddies**.

parachute

When you **parachute**, you use something that opens up and helps you float to the ground. After he jumps from the plane, Elliott will **parachute** to the ground.

people

People means more than one person. Lots of **people** came to hear Ben sing.

R

rabbit

A **rabbit** is an animal with long ears and soft fur. My pet **rabbit** likes to hop.

rocket

A **rocket** is something that flies in space. A hundred years ago, no one believed we would send a **rocket** to the Moon.

rover

A **rover** is something that moves from one place to another. The **rover** moved across the Moon's surface.

S

says

Says means tells. Mom **says** that Dad will be home soon.

sky

The **sky** is the air above the ground. I saw a plane fly high in the **sky**.

stories

A **story** is writing that tells what happens to people or to other characters. My grandma tells **stories** about what she did when she was a girl.

stubborn

If you are **stubborn**, that means you don't change your mind easily. My little sister can be **stubborn** when she wants her way.

T

teacher

A **teacher** is a person who teaches others. My mother is a math **teacher**.

Texas

Texas is a state in the United States of America. We like to visit our grandpa in **Texas**.

told

Told means said something to someone. My friend **told** me a funny joke today.

Tomás Rivera

Tomás Rivera was a writer and a teacher. **Tomás Rivera** began writing when he was a young boy.

travel

To **travel** means to go and visit another place. Next summer we are going to **travel** to South America.

troubles

Trouble is something that makes it hard to know what to do. That place has had many **troubles** over the years.

tunnel

A **tunnel** goes under ground or water to help people get from one place to another. They drove through a **tunnel** to get to the city.

V

vegetables

A **vegetable** is a plant or a part of a plant that you can eat. You should eat **vegetables** because they are good for you.

Acknowledgments

The Big Trip written and illustrated by Valeri Gorbachev. Copyright © 2004 by Valeri Gorbachev. Reprinted by permission of Philomel Books, a Division of Penguin Young Readers Group, a member of Penguin Group (USA) Inc. All rights reserved.

"Elephant, Elephant" from *The Sweet and Sour Animal Book* by Langston Hughes. Copyright © 1994 by Ramona Bass and Arnold Rampersad, Administrators of the Estate of Langston Hughes. Reprinted by permission of Oxford University Press and Harold Ober Associates, Inc.

"Funny Bunny," originally published as "Here's Bunny," from *Ring A Ring O' Roses: Finger Plays for Pre-School Children*. Published by Flint Public Library. Reprinted by permission of Flint Public Library.

Where Does Food Come From? by Shelley Rotner and Gary Goss, photographs by Shelley Rotner. Text copyright © 2006 by Shelley Rotner and Gary Goss. Photographs copyright © 2006 by Shelley Rotner. Reprinted by permission of Millbrook Press, a division of Lerner Publishing Group. All rights reserved.

Credits

Photo Credits

Placement Key: (t) top, (b) bottom, (r) right, (l) left, (bg) background, (fg) foreground, (i) inset

TOC 8a ©Ariel Skelley/Age FotoStock America, Inc.; **TOC 8b** ©John Warden/Stone/Getty Images; **9** inset © 1996 C Squared Studios; **10** (t) ©Jupterimages/ BananaStock/Alamy; **11** (b) ©NASA/Getty Images; (tl) ©MAXIM MARMUR/Staff/AFP/Getty Images; (tr) ©Corbis; (cl) ©NASA/CORBIS; (cr) ©NASA / Science Faction/Getty Images; (bl) ©Sean Sexton Collection/CORBIS; (br) ©NASA/Corbis; **12** ©Stocktrek/Corbis; (tl) Corbis; (tc) StockTrek; (tr) Digital Stock/NASA; (bl) Getty/Digital Vision; (br) Corbis; **13** NASA; **14** ©Courtesy of Steve Swinburne; **14-15** ©NASA-Apollo/Science Faction/Getty Images; **16-17** ©Ctein/Getty Images; **18** ©NASA-Apollo/Science Faction/ Getty Images; **19** ©NASA/Science Source/ Photo Researchers; **20** ©NASA/Stringer/Time & Life Pictures/Getty Images; **21** ©NASA/ Photo Researchers, Inc.; **22-23** ©Keystone/ Stringer/Getty Images; **24** ©NASA; **25** © MPI/ Stringer/Hulton Archive/Getty Images; **26-27** ©NASA; **28** ©NASA; **29** ©NASA; **30** ©NASA; **31** ©Corbis; **32-33** ©Brand X/SuperStock; **34-35** ©Robert Karpa/Masterfile; **35** (inset) ©NASA-Apollo/Science Faction/Getty Images; **44-45** (bkgd) ©NASA/Roger Ressmeyer/ Corbis; **46** (tl) ©Bettmann/Corbis; (b) ©Time Life Pictures/Getty Images; (tr) ©Robert Mora/ Getty Entertainment/Getty Images; **46-47** (bkgd) ©Stockbyte/Getty Images; **47** (cr) ©Banana Stock; **48** ©PhotoDisc; **49** ©World Perspectives/ Getty Images; **52** (t) ©Tony Freeman/Photo Edit; (b) ©Richard Hutchings/Corbis; **53** (tl) ©Ariel Skelley/Taxi/Getty Images; (tr) ©Ariel Skelley/ Getty Images; (cr) ©Dave Nagel/Taxi/ Getty Images; (cl) ©Tim Graham/Getty Images; (bl)

Illustration